BIG BOOKS
FOR LITTLE ONES

I can tell the time

written by Brenda Apsley
illustrated by Annabel Spenceley
cover by Jo Berriman

Time is how long it takes things to happen.

What time do you get up?

What time do you go to bed?

What time is it now?

Let's learn more about time . . .

It takes a long time
to build a house of blocks.

It takes a short time
to knock it down.

It takes a long time
for gelatin to set.

It takes a short time
to eat it!

It takes a long time
to blow up a balloon.

It takes a very short time
to pop it.

It takes a very short time
to say your name.

It takes a longer time
to write it.

JAMES

Time tells us when things happen.

Here is the nine o'clock news

DOG SHOW 3pm

What time is the next bus due?

At two o'clock.

What time shall I meet you?

Half past ten.

10

Clocks and watches help us measure time.

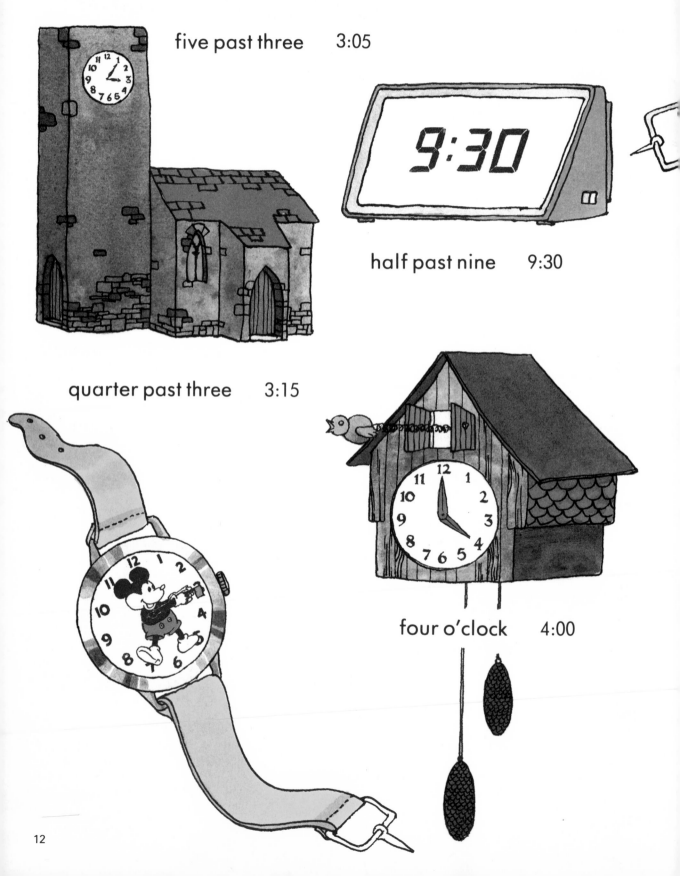

five past three   3:05

half past nine   9:30

quarter past three   3:15

four o'clock   4:00

quarter to twelve   11:45

half past seven   7:30

ten to three   2:50

eleven o'clock   11:00

Look at a clock or watch now.
What time is it?

A second is a very small measure of time.

A second is the time it takes to sneeze.

A second is the time it takes to blink.

A second is the time it takes to clap your hands.

Could you run a mile in a second?
Or bake a cake?
Could you wink in a second?

**There are 60 seconds in a minute.
A minute is a small measure of time.**

A minute is the time
it takes to put on your coat.

A minute is the time
it takes to wash your hands.

An egg will boil in 3 minutes.

A record on the radio lasts about 2 minutes.

Could you eat a hamburger in a minute?

Could you have a bath in a minute?

There are 60 minutes in an hour.
An hour is a longer measure of time.

It takes an hour to wash and dry your hair.

A soccer match lasts an hour and a half.

It takes about an hour to do the shopping.

It takes about half an hour to eat a very large ice cream.

How many hours do you sleep at night?
Could you build a snowman in an hour?

There are 24 hours in a day.
A day is a long measure of time.

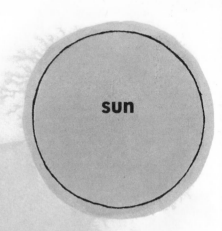

sun

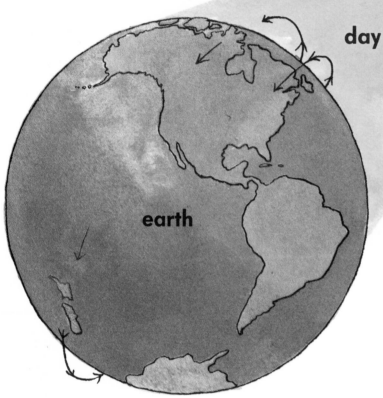

day

earth

night

Our world spins around
once every day.

When our part of the world
faces the sun we have daytime.

When our part of the world
faces away from the sun we have night.

When do you sleep?
Night or day?

When do you see stars
in the sky?
Night or day?

When do you play?
Night or day?

There are different parts of a day.

morning

afternoon

evening

night

When do you eat breakfast?
Morning or evening?

When do you watch television?

What time of the day is it NOW?

23

There are seven days in a week.

Each day has a different name.

Say the days of the week:

Monday
Tuesday
Wednesday
Thursday
Friday
Saturday
Sunday

What day is it today?

How many days in the week
do you go to playgroup or school?

Say the names of the days.

Which two days do we call the weekend?

A week is a long measure of time.

When will the clock be ready?

In a week.

LAST TWO WEEKS OF SALE!

THREE WEEK STRIKE ENDS

How long are you going to be away on vacation?

Two weeks.

There are four weeks in a month.
There are twelve months in a year.

Say the months of the year.

January

February

March

April

May

June

July

August

September

October

November

December

28

In which month is your birthday?
In which month do we celebrate Christmas?
What month are we in NOW?

Do you know how many days each month has?
January has 31 days
February has 28 days, and 29 in a leap year
March has 31 days
April has 30 days
May has 31 days
June has 30 days
July has 31 days
August has 31 days
September has 30 days
October has 31 days
November has 30 days
December has 31 days

This rhyme will help you remember:

Thirty days hath September, April, June and November. All the rest have thirty-one excepting February alone, which has twenty-eight days clear, and twenty-nine in each leap year.

A year is a long measure of time.
There are 365 days in most years, but 366 in leap years.

A birthday marks another year of your age.
How many years old are you?
How many years old is this child?

Which year were you born in?
Which year is it NOW?

How old are you?

I'm eight years old.

When did you start school?

A year ago.

When do you start at junior school?

Next year.

A calendar helps us divide up the year into days, weeks and months. It tells us the date.

Look at this page from a calendar.

1983			JUNE	
SUNDAY	MONDAY	TUESDAY	WEDNESDAY	T
			1	
5	6	7	8	
12	13	14	15	
19	20	21	22	
26	27	28	29	

What year does the calendar show?
What month does it show?
What day does it show?

1983

DAY	FRIDAY	SATURDAY
	3	4
	10	11
	17	18
3	24	25
0		

What is the date today?
Look at a calendar or diary if you don't know.

Can you tell the time?

What time do the clocks here show?
Remember, the long hand points to the minutes,
and the short hand points to the hours.

two o'clock/2:00 or three o'clock/3:00?

half past seven/7:30 or half past eight/8:30?

ten to three/2:50 or quarter past ten/10:15?

quarter past nine/9:15 or quarter to three/2:45?

six o'clock/6:00 or half past twelve/12:30?

ten past twelve/12:10 or two o'clock/2:00?

five past three/3:05 or quarter past one/1:15?

Look at a watch or clock.
What time is it?

Draw in the hands on the clock face:

Write in the digital time:

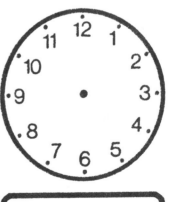

35

What time do these things happen?

41

43